Victory Over the Lying Spirit

DS VOLUME 22

Bishop Climate Irungu

Copyright © 2016 by Bishop Climate Ministries

All rights reserved. No part of this publication may be reproduced, distributed or transmitted in any form or by any means, including photocopying, recording, or other electronic or mechanical methods, without the prior written permission of the publisher, except in the case of brief quotations embodied in critical reviews and certain other noncommercial uses permitted by copyright law. For permission requests, write to the publisher, addressed "Attention: Permissions Coordinator," at the address below.

Bishop Climate Ministries
PO Box 67884
London, England SE5 9JJ
www.bishopclimate.org
Email: prayer@bishopclimate.org
Tel: +44 7984 115900 (UK)
Tel: +44 207 738 3668 (UK)
Tel: +732 444 8943 (USA)

Contents

Micaiah Prophesies Against Ahab 5

What is a Lying Spirit? 9

Five Ways the Lying Spirit Can Attack You 18

Three Signs of a Lying Spirit 29

15 Prayer Points For Victory Over the Lying Spirit 31

What Can I Expect? 36

SCRIPTURAL REFERENCE

Micaiah Prophesies Against Ahab

So the king of Israel brought together the prophets—about four hundred men—and asked them, "Shall I go to war against Ramoth Gilead, or shall I refrain?"

"Go," they answered, "for the Lord will give it into the king's hand."

But Jehoshaphat asked, "Is there no longer a prophet of the Lord here whom we can inquire of?"

The king of Israel answered Jehoshaphat, "There is still one prophet through whom we can inquire of the Lord, but I hate him because he never prophesies anything good about me, but always bad. He is Micaiah son of Imlah."

"The king should not say such a thing," Jehoshaphat replied.

So the king of Israel called one of his officials and said, "Bring Micaiah son of Imlah at once."

Dressed in their royal robes, the king of Israel and Jehoshaphat king of Judah were sitting on their thrones at the threshing floor by the entrance of the gate of Samaria, with all the prophets prophesying before them. Now Zedekiah son of Kenaanah had made iron horns and he declared, "This is what the Lord says: 'With these you will gore the Arameans until they are destroyed.'"

All the other prophets were prophesying the same thing. "Attack Ramoth Gilead and be victorious," they said, "for the Lord will give it into the king's hand."

The messenger who had gone to summon Micaiah said to him, "Look, the other prophets without exception are predicting success for the king. Let your word agree with theirs, and speak favorably."

But Micaiah said, "As surely as the Lord lives, I can tell him only what the Lord tells me."

VICTORY OVER THE LYING SPIRIT | 7

When he arrived, the king asked him, "Micaiah, shall we go to war against Ramoth Gilead, or not?"

"Attack and be victorious," he answered, "for the Lord will give it into the king's hand."

The king said to him, "How many times must I make you swear to tell me nothing but the truth in the name of the Lord?"

Then Micaiah answered, "I saw all Israel scattered on the hills like sheep without a shepherd, and the Lord said, 'These people have no master. Let each one go home in peace.'"

The king of Israel said to Jehoshaphat, "Didn't I tell you that he never prophesies anything good about me, but only bad?"

Micaiah continued, "Therefore hear the word of the Lord: I saw the Lord sitting on his throne with all the multitudes of heaven standing around him on his right and on his left. And the Lord said, 'Who will entice Ahab into attacking Ramoth Gilead and going to his death there?'

"One suggested this, and another that. Finally, a spirit came forward, stood before the Lord and said, 'I will entice him.'

"'By what means?' the Lord asked.

"'I will go out and be a deceiving spirit in the mouths of all his prophets,' he said.

"'You will succeed in enticing him,' said the Lord. 'Go and do it.'

"So now the Lord has put a deceiving spirit in the mouths of all these prophets of yours. The Lord has decreed disaster for you." (1 Kings 22: 6 – 23)

PART ONE

What is a Lying Spirit?

> **But Jehoshaphat asked, 'Is there no longer a prophet of the Lord here whom we can inquire of?' (1 Kings 22:7)**

When the King of Israel called together the prophets to ask if he should go up to war, 400 of them were in agreement and said, "Yes go, for God will give you victory!"

Surely it would have been reasonable to believe they had heard from the Lord as they were all in agreement. But the King of Judah, King Jehoshaphat, knew that something wasn't right. He needed a prophet of the Lord, somebody that was hearing from God. These 400 men were just there to encourage but they were not walking in the right spirit. Jehoshaphat knew that if he only listened to what they were saying, he could be walking into a death trap.

If you want to stop going through the trouble you have been facing then you are going to have to realize that you have to stop listening to what you want to hear, and listen to what God is saying.

The King of Israel said that there was one prophet of the Lord they could call on but he hated him because he never prophesied anything good, only bad.

Sometimes we can be so headstrong on wanting something that we only hear what we want to hear. God is trying to say, "No, not yet, just wait, be patient, hold on." But we don't want to hear that. We want to hear "Yes" we want to hear "You can have it now!" Too many people are getting into trouble this way;

they play themselves right into the hands of this lying spirit.

> Micaiah continued, "Therefore hear the word of the Lord: I saw the Lord sitting on his throne with all the multitudes of heaven standing around him on his right and on his left. And the Lord said, 'Who will entice Ahab into attacking Ramoth Gilead and going to his death there?' "One suggested this, and another that. Finally, a spirit came forward, stood before the Lord and said, 'I will entice him.'
>
> "'By what means?' the Lord asked. "'I will go out and be a deceiving spirit in the mouths of all his prophets,' he said.
> "'You will succeed in enticing him,' said the Lord. 'Go and do it. "So now the Lord has put a deceiving spirit in the mouths of all these prophets of yours. The Lord has decreed disaster for you."
>
> (1 Kings 22:19-23)

What happened? These prophets were not speaking the truth, but a lying spirit was at work in order to speak to the king of Israel and cause him to go up to his death.

This is how people die prematurely, they get into a bad marriage, a bad career, a bad situation, because they didn't really want to hear what God was saying, instead they listened to what sounded right or what sounded good at that time.

There are some unprovoked battles that can lead you to your death, spiritual death, marriage death, financial death, etc.

It happened to King Josiah:

After all this, when Josiah had set the temple in order, Necho king of Egypt went up to fight at Carchemish on the Euphrates, and Josiah marched out to meet him in battle. But Necho sent messengers to him, saying, "What quarrel is there, king of Judah, between you and me? It is not you I am attacking at this time, but the house with which I am at war. God has told me to hurry; so stop opposing God, who is with me, or he will destroy you." Josiah, however, would not turn away from him, but disguised himself to engage him in battle. He would not listen to what Necho had said at God's command but went to fight him on the plain of Megiddo.

VICTORY OVER THE LYING SPIRIT | 13

Archers shot King Josiah, and he told his officers, "Take me away; I am badly wounded." So they took him out of his chariot, put him in his other chariot and brought him to Jerusalem, where he died. He was buried in the tombs of his ancestors, and all Judah and Jerusalem mourned for him.

(2 Kings 35:20-24)

As a believer if this spirit lies to you and you rise up against an innocent person, God will not protect you. That's why you should never involve yourself in other peoples business, because you do not know the relationship they have with God, you do not know the instruction they have from God. You may not understand what they are doing, but leave them alone.

King Josiah was someone who was prophesied about before he was born. They said that he would be a great man and rebuild the temple of God. But then he got himself involved in the wrong things by trying to fight battles that were not his, and as a result, his life was short lived. This king could have lived for a long time but there was a lying spirit pushing him in the wrong direction. There is no other spirit that has cut off so many people from good jobs, businesses, marriages, relationships and destinies like this spirit. God did not call you to fight everyone's battle. You must discern wisely and make sure you are not enticed to fight a losing battle. In short, don't try to defend what God is trying to kill or wipe out because at that point you take the nature of the devil or the enemy of God. And down you will go. So examine yourself.

This spirit will come and entice you to fight somebody, to get involved in unnecessary battles. Some people keep picking on others, but just leave them alone; they have nothing to do with you. If two people have an issue with each other, why do you want to get involved? That is foolishness.

> Like one who grabs a stray dog by the ears is someone who rushes into a quarrel not their own.
>
> (Proverbs 26:17)

When you grab a dog by its ears you're putting yourself in a position to be bit, you are going to get hurt. (Remember a dog's ears are flexible and it can easily turn its head to bite you).

How many of you want to live long and do what God has called you to do? There are many people that love God, but this spirit comes and they start fighting people they shouldn't fight.

There are some things that you have to leave alone because they are unnecessary. I will say it again, unless it's affecting you, keep away.

Sometimes there are some situations I see happening but I stay out of it, not because I don't care, but because I know the devil just wants to trap me.

One day I met someone who was having one court case after another, and as she was speaking to me I recalled what used to happen in my family. My mother and father were always going to court over different things, but the only person benefiting was the lawyer. As this woman spoke to me I realized what the problem was, something had been speaking to her.

Here she was thinking it was her own mind, her own understanding, but something was speaking to her causing her to be in court every week.

I told that lady that there was a lying spirit speaking to her all the time and because of it she has been pursuing this case that was a lie. Somebody went to a witch doctor and sent a lying spirit to her, to waste all her time and resources on the courts. For 15 years she had been pursuing something that never brought any results. And how much did she gain? She used to be a very wealthy woman but now all she has is files, chasing this and chasing that.

When this type of thing happens, you can never move on with your life, you can never enjoy life because you're always filing this or filing that. A lying spirit can even physically inflict you or those around you just to cause delay. So the judge keeps prolonging the case because of headache or sickness or other issues, telling you to come back next week, he keeps pushing it off. And then it never ends.

I read an article in the newspaper the other day about a man who spent £13,000 in court just to fight a £60 fine. He said he didn't care how much he had to spend; he wanted to prove a point. At the end he won his case, but at what cost?

Sometimes a spirit can be assigned into your life for you to make a wrong financial decision. You need to know when it's the right time to pull out.

The only thing you can do to stop this spirit is to pray and seek the wisdom of God. That's it, there's no physical way to stop it. Even Jesus said that some things only go through fasting and prayer. (Mark 9:29)

Prayer is important. That's why a prayerful church is a powerful church. You must get connected to a prayer team, get connected to a prayer church or a ministry like ours. Get rooted; enroll yourself in different prayer programs. And if you really want permanent results then enroll yourself in one of our online deliverance programs.

PART TWO

Five Ways the Lying Spirit Can Attack You

1. MARRIAGE

A lying spirit is one of the main causes behind divorce. A lying spirit will use your past against you; it will tell you that your husband/wife is just like the person you used to date. It can twist circumstances to make it look suspicious, to cause doubt. But remember every situation can be looked at in different ways. How you look at it determines how you see it. Sometimes a little hill can become a big mountain by listening to the devil. A lying spirit can cause you to interpret things in the wrong way. They can harass you and cause you to believe things and see things that aren't true. It puts doubt in you and you begin to mistrust. Then you begin sowing that in your marriage and it can lead to other things, a lot of strife, unhappiness, etc.

2. HEALTH

A lying spirit will tell you that you have this disease and that disease. There can be nothing wrong with you, but you believe it and then suddenly that thing begins to develop. One lady went to the hospital once because she felt ill. When they ran tests on her they told her she was HIV positive. The lady knew that there was no way that was possible, she refused because she knew that she was still a virgin and had never exposed herself to a virus either sexually or physically. She told them to run the test again. When they did, it came back negative. So what was that? It was a lying spirit. All what it needed was for that woman to give in to fear and believe what the test results said, then that disease would begin operating in her life. This spirit works alongside the spirit of fear. You may have some family members who have died from cancer or another disease, and this spirit will come and lie to you to make you believe that you have it. You start seeing things that are not there. Remember what you think you ultimately become.

Use the law of denial to overcome this. Deny those issues, just say NO. Refuse to accept it in your life and it will go.

Until recently, many people in the past have died in disgrace and shame thinking they had AIDS, yet it was actually cancer. Technology has proven so. Whatsoever wants to bring shame and disgrace in your life must die by fire!

3. CAREER

A lot of people are miserable, working in a career that they shouldn't be in due to this lying spirit. How does it happen? Somehow you heard that you should go for a certain career, maybe your family or your friends pushed you into it, and now your working at a job that you hate because it's not for you. Other times you can be at the right place, but because of a lying spirit, you pick up and leave everything for something else that is not right.

4. FINANCIAL

A lying spirit will tell you to put all your money in something that is doomed to failure. You think because you keep hearing these voices, you keep having this nudge that it must be a sign or a voice from God, but if you're not in tune with the Holy Spirit, it's going to lead you down the wrong path. This spirit is so dangerous, especially when activated through witchcraft or sorcery.

It's this demon that is used in scams. I have met people who have lost hundreds of thousands through Internet scams, money scams, etc. They tell you that you have won such and such an amount, or someone has died and you are the sole heir, there is millions of dollars in an account just waiting for you. Then they tell you that all you need to do is to pay for insurance, courier, release fees, storage fees, etc. And once they make that contact with you and you send your details, they use them to infuse this lying spirit and they begin to monitor you and take charge of your life. You end up believing this lie without limit. Even you start seeing it as if its God's plan and little by little they defraud you. You borrow, you use all your money, and even go into debt, living in false hope that big money is coming. Sometimes they even infuse love to confuse you. Days turn to months, months to years, always hoping that this money is coming, and suddenly you are unable to pay your bills, keep up with your payments, your family is torn apart, friendships are broken. The more you are isolated the more you become vulnerable, losing everything. And this will not leave you until you are dead. If this is you, you must seek immediate deliverance. I have been able to help many but others were too convinced through this spirit, finding themselves homeless, bankrupt, and sadly end up dying of a broken heart, depression or committing suicide. You must get delivered and get out before it's too late.

5. DESTINY

A lying spirit can come and cause you to make wrong decisions that lead you to your death. It can cause you to pick up and leave what God has for you to go for something entirely different. A lying spirit is very dangerous because you can walk out of something that God has for you only to get disappointed in the end. I've seen many people walk out of golden opportunities that God had for them because a spirit lied to them. They thought they had a bad feeling and so they dropped it only to regret it for the rest of their lives. I have seen people who started hearing voices telling them that a certain person in their working place didn't like them or that they were a witch; other voices will speak and lie against people who have your best interest at heart, they want to help you but in turn, you rise against them, burning the bridges that you could have used to cross tomorrow. A lying spirit is the cause of many mental illnesses and psychotic problems.

HOW TO AVOID THIS SPIRIT

The devil can use this spirit to cut your life off, to destroy your marriage, to destroy your health, to destroy your career, to destroy your destiny.

It can speak to you through dreams using familiar faces to cause chaos. It can speak to you through your subconscious, through your mind, even audible voices, pretending to be from God. It can even speak to you through other people (that's why you must check your associations). But I pray you mature spiritually so you can see it from far and recognize it for what it is. That's why you need to join the special prayer program that I have to clear your mind and build a permanent defense against this spirit.

So how do you avoid this?

Most people are an easy target for a lying spirit because they only want to hear what they want to hear. It leads to self-deception, which can be very dangerous. You start hearing things that aren't from God, because that's what you want to hear. But what do you want? Do you want something that will please you now but lead to disaster? Or do you want the truth that will set you free?

The King of Israel only wanted to do what his mind was telling him; little did he know that the voices and thoughts he was hearing in his mind were a lying spirit. And the same spirit had infected all the prophets he was listening to as well. He was meant to hear only what was pleasing to his ears; he didn't want to hear the truth. And that was to his destruction. Today any lying spirit that wants you to think what it wants to accomplish in your life, I command it to stop now!

If you want to overcome this spirit, then you must be determined. Say, "God, if the answer is no then I'm okay with it, so long as I know it's you. And I know that you have my best interest as heart, so I trust you that you have something better in store for me. But I am willing to wait; I am willing to endure your discipline, because I want your very best!"

> Then David said to Abiathar the priest, the son of Ahimelek, "Bring me the ephod." Abiathar brought it to him, and David inquired of the Lord, "Shall I pursue this raiding party? Will I overtake them?"
> "Pursue them," he answered. "You will certainly overtake them and succeed in the rescue."
>
> (1 Sam 30: 7-8)

When you are seeking a new venture in your life, maybe a new career, a marriage, a business venture, or you are a facing a legal battle, etc. do you seek the Lord first before making a decision?

The Bible says to commit your ways to Him and He shall direct your paths (Proverbs 3:6). That means being open to what God is saying and willing to change direction if necessary.

You need to know when God is speaking and when he is not speaking. Some people get excited and think God is speaking but he's not.

Avoid abusing the term, "The Lord said…"

Understand that you are a spirit man, you have a soul and you live in a body. 99% of what you feel, hear, and think, is coming out of your soul. But too often people have bad habits of thinking it is the Lord. So they are always going around saying the Lord said this, the Lord told me to drink this, or eat that, but in fact it has nothing to do with God. And you become an easy target, because the devil knows that he can just drop one thought and you won't even hesitate because you have programmed yourself to believe that it's from God. I've seen people go around saying, "Oh the Lord told me to go and drink some juice". I'm not saying that he can't do that, but the majority of the time people are taking advantage of it when it's not God at all.

PART THREE

Three Signs of a Lying Spirit

1. PRIDE

When a lying spirit comes and lies to you, you become proud.

Some women are completely in love with themselves; they think everything is about them and that every man wants them. But it's just a lying spirit; it has made them so proud. Other times you find people in the working place that think they are better than everyone else. They go around with big mouths always talking about themselves, but when you look at their results there is nothing to show; they are just boasting. At least if they know the truth they can improve themselves, but instead they remain self-deceived.

2. SELF-DECEPTION

People with a lying spirit don't want to listen to anybody, they know what they know and what they know is right. They are convinced that they are right and their mind is already made up.

3. QUARRELS

When you see people always quarrelling, they have a lying spirit at work in their lives. Don't fight other people's battles. If the person you are fighting is innocent God will not help you. Sometimes people are suffering because they did something bad. Leave them alone and keep your peace.

15 PRAYER POINTS FOR

Victory Over the Lying Spirit

Before you pray, remember to put on the full armor of God according to Ephesians 6:10-18, touching each part of your body as you say it.

> *Repeat with me: "I put on the full armor of God. The helmet of salvation upon my head, the breastplate of righteousness in its place, the belt of truth around my waist, my feet shod with the readiness of the gospel of peace, taking the shield of faith in my left hand and the sword of the spirit in my right".*

In the Name of Jesus:

1. I take authority over every lying spirit that has been assigned to cause destruction, sickness and disease, I bind you and I rebuke you!

2. Every lying spirit assigned to cause trouble in my life, in my working place, I bind you, I rebuke you, and I command you to die by fire!

3. I take authority over every lying spirit that has been assigned to cause failure, premature death, discouragement, failure of my business, relationships, marriage, health, I rebuke you, I bind you, I command you to die by fire!

4. Every lying spirit that I have inherited from my father's house, from my mother's house, I command it to die by fire!

VICTORY OVER THE LYING SPIRIT | 33

5. Every lying spirit that has been causing me to make mistakes, to make bad decisions, financial mistakes, marriage mistakes, health mistakes, career mistakes, I rebuke you. Die by fire!

6. Every lying spirit that has been assigned to drive me to bankruptcy, to drive me to death, to drive me to sickness, die by fire!

7. Every lying spirit that has been sent to me in order to cause death in my life, finances, spiritual life, I command it to die by fire!

8. Every lying spirit that has been assigned over my marriage in order to cause doubt and suspicion, to manipulate circumstances in the wrong way, I bind you, I rebuke you, I command you to die by fire!

9. Every lying spirit that has been enticing me to fight other people, to get involved in battles that are not my own, I rebuke it in Jesus name!

10. Every lying spirit that has caused me to get into the wrong career, I bind it, I rebuke it, I command it to die by fire!

11. Every lying spirit that has made me enter bad financial deals, to lose all of my money, I command it to die by fire!

12. Every lying spirit that wants to keep me involved in court cases and legal battles in order to waste all of my resources, energy, and time, I command it to stop! I bind it, I rebuke it, and I command it to die by fire!

13. Every lying spirit that wants to cause me to forfeit my destiny, to walk away on the good plans that God has for me, I bind you, and I rebuke you, die by fire!

14. I shut every lying voice of the devil! I refuse to listen anymore! I declare blessed are those who trust in the Lord and turn not aside to lies in Jesus name!

VICTORY OVER THE LYING SPIRIT | 35

15. Today I declare that I do not have a spirit of fear but a spirit of love and a sound mind.

CONCLUSION

What Can I Expect?

So now that you have your prayer points you need to understand that deliverance is not a onetime event but a process and you need to be consistent if you are going to destroy the enemies in your life. Let's look at a few things you can expect while going through your deliverance.

Firstly, expect to be set free and for peace to return back into your life. The Bible says that those who wait for the Lord shall not be ashamed. Also, start expecting God to give you a testimony, just like everyone else who has gone through our deliverance program.

There are some key steps you can follow to ensure you are doing everything properly in order to obtain your desired goals. (These are in addition to your daily prayer points listed in this book)

1. Locate the area of your need

According to what your situation may be, you need to identify the particular area or areas, which are most dire.

2. Find out what the Word of God says regarding that area

Select the appropriate scriptures promising you what you desire and meditate upon them. Write them on your walls where you can see them. Even if it means writing it on yourself so you won't forget to recite them during the day. Do whatever it takes but make sure you are replaying them in your mind daily.

3. <u>Go through a special prayer in one of the following ways while expecting your deliverance</u>

· 3 day Night Vigil at the Sanctuary (i.e. praying and confessing the Word from 10 pm to 5 am for 3 nights in a row)

· 3 Day Fast (i.e. praying, fasting, and confessing the Word daily from 6 am to 6 pm for 3 days. Alternatively you can fast straight through the 3 days only breaking for communion)

· 3-Day Fast Prayer Vigil at the Sanctuary (i.e. praying, fasting, and confessing the Word daily from 10 am to 6 pm for 3 days. Again you can fast continually for 3 days apart from communion)

· 3 + Days Dry Fast (i.e. praying, fasting, and confessing the Word for 3 or more days without taking food or drink). Please note: This should only be done under pastoral recommendation.

4. Pray aggressively while believing that you receive your deliverance

Hebrews 11:6 says, *"we must believe that He is and that He is a rewarder of them that diligently seek Him".*

5. Make any adjustments in your life and repent as the Holy Spirit leads

You have to make sure that you are not leaving any open doors for the enemy to regain access in your life.

6. This is the most crucial step. You must sow your seed to seal your deliverance

Most people sow consecutive seeds, giving it the same name according to their expectation from God regarding their deliverance. To truly succeed in spiritual warfare you have to be a sower. The Bible says in Deut 16:16 to "never appear before God empty handed". So as you are expecting to receive something from God you need to be giving back something to Him as well.

7. <u>Lastly, prepare yourself for your miracle physically and spiritually</u>

Be vigorous in attending service as much as possible in order to receive the ministration of the Word and the laying on of the hands by the man of God. Also, attend your deliverance sessions regularly if you have been assigned to a mentor.

Bishop Climate Ministries
P.O. Box 67884, London, SE5 9JJ
England, United Kingdom
Tel: +44 7984 115900
Email: partners@bishopclimate.org

Yes Bishop! I declare 'Blessed are those who make the Lord their trust and turn not aside to lies' (Psalms 40:4) So I sow my seed of £40.40 to shut every voice of the devil.

I have enclosed my special seed of deliverance
£ _____

Please also send me: Anointed Oil for Total Victory

Here is my Prayer request covering the 7 areas I desire the Lord to manifest His Miracles in my life:

_____

_____

_____

_____

_____

(Continued on Back)

42 | BISHOP CLIMATE IRUNGU

Name:

_____

Address:

_____

_____

_____

Telephone:

_____

Email:

_____

NOTE: You can also sow your special seed SAFELY &
SECURELY online via www.bishopclimate.org

ABOUT THE MINISTRY

Bishop Climate Ministries is the Healing & Deliverance Ministry founded by Bishop Climate under the anointing and direction of the Holy Spirit. God has anointed Bishop Climate with incredible power to set the captives free. Many people who were unable to get deliverance anywhere else find their freedom as they attend special deliverance sessions conducted through this ministry. The vision of Bishop Climate Ministries is to reach over 1 billion people with the message of deliverance and prosperity, especially in understanding the things of the spirit. Many people are bound because of lack of knowledge and one of the goals of this ministry is to set people free through education.

A PERSONAL NOTE FROM THE AUTHOR

Child of God I want you to know how much I appreciate you and how special you are to me. That is why God keeps giving me the wisdom to write these books at such a time as this. He sees your heart and wants you to experience the abundant life that Jesus died for. And so do I. Your support for our ministry is crucial and I hope that you will always continue to lift us up in prayer to God.

I want to take this opportunity to encourage you to partner with us at Bishop Climate Ministries. Hundreds have testified of the miracles that have taken place in their life just as a result of sowing into this ministry and I want you to be able to experience that 100 fold return Jesus spoke about regarding sowing seed into good ground. The Bible says in Proverbs 11:24 *"One person gives freely, yet gains even more; another withholds unduly, but comes to poverty"*.

VICTORY OVER THE LYING SPIRIT | 45

Your prayers and financial support are crucial to take this message of salvation and deliverance around the world. And as you do that you can be sure that God is going to bless you beyond your wildest imaginations. There is a 4-fold anointing that you step under when you become a partner with Bishop Climate Ministries. It is the anointing that God has put over my life and this ministry according to Isaiah 11:2. That is the anointing of Divine Direction, Divine Connections, Divine Provision and Divine Protection.

Please understand how much I value you. Your support for our ministry is so crucial and your prayers are as a pillar to us. Your partnership with this ministry is so important and that's why we are committed to praying for you daily and lifting your needs up before God. When you send in your donation please send me a prayer request as well so I can intercede on your behalf before God. I look forward to seeing you in person at our Healing and Deliverance Centre in London, England or at one of our Healing and Deliverance Miracle Crusades.

Remember this is the Ministry where the captives are set free and souls are refreshed.

Remain blessed,

Bishop Climate Irungu

MORE TITLES FROM OUR DELIVERANCE SERIES

Victory Over The Spirit Of Humiliation & Oppression
Breaking The Curse Of
Good Beginnings & Bad Endings
Victory Over Demonic Assignments
Overcoming Every Generational Hatred
Overcoming Persistent Enemies
Destroying Every Demonic Blockage
Victory Over Every Troubling Spirit
Destroying Every Spirit of Poverty & Lack
Destroying Every Demonic Covenant Over Your Life
Victory Over Every Appointment With Death
Binding the Strongman
Uprooting Every Demonic Prophecy
Victory Over Every Evil Wish
Breaking Every Demonic Spell
Overturning Every Demonic Judgment
Victory Over Every Frustrating Spirit
Destroying Every Demonic Altar
Uprooting Every Territorial Sorcerers
Victory Over Demonic Storms (Marine Spirit)
Dealing With the Spirit of Disappointment

Order Enquiries: Please call our offices or order online at www.bishopclimate.me

Bishop Climate Ministries
PO Box 67884
London, England SE5 9JJ
www.bishopclimate.org
Email: prayer@bishopclimate.org
Tel: +44 7984 115900 (UK)
Tel: +44 207 738 3668 (UK)
Tel: +732 444 8943 (USA)

Printed in Poland
by Amazon Fulfillment
Poland Sp. z o.o., Wrocław